Charlotte Dean

**Lassie, and her guardian angel**

Charlotte Dean

**Lassie, and her guardian angel**

ISBN/EAN: 9783741174216

Manufactured in Europe, USA, Canada, Australia, Japa

Cover: Foto ©Andreas Hilbeck / pixelio.de

Manufactured and distributed by brebook publishing software (www.brebook.com)

Charlotte Dean

**Lassie, and her guardian angel**

# Tales for the Young.

## LASSIE,

### AND

## Her Guardian Angel.

BY CHARLOTTE DEAN,

AUTHORESS OF "MAY TEMPLETON."

—:0:—

LONDON:
THOMAS RICHARDSON AND SON;
23, King Edward Street, City;
AND DERBY.

# CONTENTS.

## CHAPTER I.
Lassie's Home .. .. .. 5

## CHAPTER II.
Lassie's Concert .. .. .. .. 16

## CHAPTER III.
The Wolf .. .. .. .. .. 26

## CHAPTER IV.
Lassie's Friend .. .. .. .. 39

## CHAPTER V.
The Invitation .. .. .. .. 52

## CHAPTER VI.
The King's Messenger .. .. .. 67

## CHAPTER VII.
The Return Home .. .. .. .. 80

## CHAPTER VIII.
The Chapel of our Lady .. .. .. 89

## CHAPTER IX.
Conclusion .. .. .. .. .. 98

# LASSIE,

AND

### Her Guardian Angel.

---

## CHAPTER I.

Some few years ago there stood in the north-western part of London a very large old-fashioned house, which in former days had been the abode of a noble family, but had latterly been converted into a lodging-house; and up and down the broad oaken staircase, where, in days long since gone by, ladies and gentlemen of rank and fashion had been wont to tread in gay and rich attire, the children of toil were now to be seen climbing wearily up to their separate apartments, or what "we short-lived creatures call our *homes*."

Into one of these *homes* we now enter, and see a woman no longer young, but with traces of beauty still lingering on her weary face, bending over some snowy-looking needlework. At her feet sit two little girls: the elder one about eleven years of age, helping mother with some of the easier portions of the work; and the other, a tiny creature with golden hair and angel-like face, not yet seven, playing with an old doll, and singing, as she nurses, one of the "Oratory Hymns," but in a low, hushed voice, for fear of disturbing "father," a pale, haggard-looking man, sitting in a corner of the room, writing away at some law papers as though his very life depended on their being finished ere the short November day closed in.

And well he might be anxious and hurried, as not only his own daily means of subsistence, but that of others far dearer to him than self, depended chiefly on his earnings. So he wrote on from morn to eve, and often long after midnight, at badly-paid copying work, in the hope of keeping the wolf from the door. In that gloomy old chamber, though invisible to human eye, were four other dwellers, four bright Angels standing amid the gloom, keeping their silent watch. Two of these Angel-sentinels stood behind the children, listening to their hymn; the shadowy lips of the Angels were moving, as though they were joining in the sweet melody. But there is a strange difference in the expression of their angelic faces as they watch the children committed to their charge; the smile on the features of the one who watches over Effie, the elder child, is full of joy and peace, while the expression on the face of the Angel who bends over the younger is blended with pity, although full of divine love. What troubles the Angel? Is the child wilful or disobedient ? Not at all. Lassie is one of the sweetest and dearest children that ever a mother was blessed with. But alas! though nearly six years old, she has not yet received the white robe of innocence given to each of God's children in holy baptism. Poor little Lassie was still outside of the fold of the Good Shepherd. No wonder the Angel who watched her so intently wore a pitiful smile as he bent over his little charge, and spread his radiant wings so closely around her whilst she sang.

Another Angel form stood beside the busy father. On this Angel's lips no song trembled, but, stern of aspect and terrible in his angelic beauty, he pointed towards Lassie, the child who is singing so sweetly of that paradise to which she has no claim, and of that Shepherd into whose fold she has not been admitted. If the Angel standing by her father's side could clothe his sorrowful anger in human language, he would sternly assure that guilty father that should the child die unbaptized, and never behold the face of God, it were better for him that he had been drowned in the depths of the sea. The child's mother was far less to blame than the father. Brought up among rigid Calvinists, and unbaptized herself, she was ignorant of the priceless gift of which her Lassie had been so cruelly deprived. Lassie's father was a Catholic, or, to speak more correctly, *had* been a Catholic in his early boyhood, and it is now proper that we give our young readers a brief sketch of his history up to the time our little story opens.

Mr. Greenwood had not been an inmate of the old house very long. He had seen far better days. About two years previous to the time our story begins he had held an excellent position as head railway clerk at a station on the London and Brighton line; but having met with an accident while crossing the rails on a busy excursion day, he had become unfit for the post, and had since that time been earning a precarious livelihood by his present occupation of copyist. He had never been what people call a strong man, and, with nerves sadly shattered by the accident, some outdoor employment would have been better for him. But his lameness forbade this, and so he was forced to "make the best of it," as so many of earth's children have to do, and to carry his cross. Happy they who bear it patiently! Happy they who in the midst of their daily toil fix their eyes on that dear and Sacred Figure, who for their example trod the way of the cross, and is ever whispering into the ear of all those weary pilgrims that care to listen, as hour by hour perchance they all but sink beneath their burden, of the "Green Pastures," and the "Still Waters," beside which all toil and weariness shall quickly—ah, how quickly—be forgotten!

Well had it been for Samuel Greenwood had he listened to that whisper. But alas! he was barely a Catholic in name, not at all in heart or practice. But his parents dying ere he was twelve years old, he had been left in charge of an uncle, a man of no faith, and well content therefore was he if his nephew behaved with outward decorum, and earned his bread like a gentleman. This was the highest ambition of the uncle's heart. As to religion, he laughed it to scorn, more especially the Catholic religion, in which his brother, the boy's father, had lived and died.

This uncle lived in a country town, four miles from any Catholic church, and though at first, and indeed for many a month after his father's death, the boy would get up early on Sunday morning, and walk to Mass at Crawley, a neighbouring town, yet by degrees the ridicule of his uncle and cousins, and his own love of ease, gained the victory over conscience and the sweet memories of childhood, so that at last he abandoned the practice of his religion altogether, and after a year or two ceased even to offer up his morning or evening prayer.

Being a clever boy, Samuel got on nicely as far as this world goes, and after his uncle's death obtained the head clerkship at Balcombe, that prettiest of all the many pretty villages on the London and Brighton line of railway. At the age of twenty-five he married a young girl for the sake of her winning face and gentle manners. She made him an unselfish and affectionate wife: but Susan Markham had been brought up in Scotland, among Calvinists, whose gloomy tenets had so depressed her sunny nature, that on growing up she had turned her back on the sect altogether, and, being wholly ignorant of the true faith, had become a careless, worldly girl, with little thought of anything beyond dress and amusement. Her early marriage, however, to a man for whom she had conceived a deep attachment, brought to light the hidden virtues of a naturally generous and warm-hearted disposition, and she made an excellent wife and devoted mother.

Her first child, a girl, was born two years after her marriage. The old nurse who attended the baby and its mother being, most providentially, a pious Catholic, easily obtained permission from the child's easy-tempered father to allow the infant to be baptized at one of the Catholic churches in Brighton. Lassie was not born till Effie was six years old, and alas! there was then no good Catholic nurse at hand to obtain for the helpless little one the priceless gift bestowed upon her sister.

Mr. Greenwood had become one of those pitiable creatures who forget God altogether, and his wife was equally forgetful of the same great Being. She had her baby duly registered by the district office appointed for the purpose, and she called the child *Lassie*, in remembrance of an old schoolmate. Thus it came to pass that poor little Lassie, though registered according to law among the children of this world, had no name in the heavenly register, and no inheritance among the children of light.

Neither of the children has the least idea of the peril in which Lassie stands; but one might fancy, from the strangely sad and beseeching expression of her large soft eyes, as she raises them now and then to her sister's face, that the child is silently entreating Effie to obtain for her something or another of which she stands in need, but to which she cannot give a name. That pleading look often puzzled Effie, but it did not puzzle Lassie's Angel,—he knew full well the meaning of it,—and catching its reflection upon his own bright face, he raised his star-like eyes to heaven, and gazed into the face of its Queen. He utters no petition, not even an *Ave*, but the Queen of Angels understands that silent prayer.

But our young readers will perhaps wonder how it came to pass that Lassie, the unbaptized child without a guardian angel, or anyone to point out to her or her sister the road that leads to heaven, should have been singing one of the Oratory hymns on the day we first introduced her to them. This question we will answer in our next chapter.

## CHAPTER II.

### LASSIE'S CONCERT.

When Mr. and Mrs. Greenwood were living in the country they had more leisure, the latter especially, to devote to their children, and both having received a good education, they were able, as well as willing, to impart this knowledge to their children. Lassie was too young to learn much before the accident to her father obliged them all to leave their pretty cottage, and move to London; but Effie could read and write very fairly for her age, and had also learned a little history and geography, as well as arithmetic. But neither she nor her little sister had received any sort of religious instruction till they came to live in London, and then they received it only by what some people would call *accident*.

How they came to receive religious instruction we shall now relate. One afternoon, a few months before the opening of our story, Mrs. Greenwood sent her two children out to play for an hour in a quiet, old-fashioned square, about a quarter of a mile distant from their home, as they sadly missed the lanes and meadows of Balcombe, in which they used to ramble about, and were looking pale and listless from want of fresh air.

It was a cold day in March, and as their jackets were almost threadbare, it was no easy matter for them to keep warm, even by chasing each other about the square. To return home earlier than usual was proposed by Effie, and they were proceeding quickly on the way thither, when, on turning the corner of a narrow street, they were arrested by the sound of children's voices singing.

The sound proceeded from an unpretending-looking building, with a cross over the porch, and the outer door standing partly open.

"Oh, Effie, darling!" cried Lassie, who had a sort of passion for music, "how pretty it sounds! Pray stop and listen; or perhaps they would let us go in, as the door is open."

"But we have no money," said Effie, who had already learnt that few pleasures in London are to be obtained without it; "and besides," added she, thoughtfully, "father and mother might not like us to go in."

"Oh, then, let us run home and ask them, and perhaps we might get back again before the concert is over." And suiting the action to her words, off ran Lassie, followed by her sister, equally anxious to obtain the desired permission.

Mrs. Greenwood looked up surprised from her needlework as the eager children flew into the room, and on hearing their request, nodded across to her husband, asking what he thought of it.

"Oh," answered Mr. Greenwood, looking up wearily from his papers, "let them go by all means, if it makes them happy; they sadly need a little amusement, poor pets, for it's dreary sitting here day after day; and there can be no harm in the place at this time of day, and in that quiet street. Some juvenile concert, I suppose, and I can spare a shilling for once in a way to give them a treat. So here goes, little ones; run off and enjoy yourselves." And tossing the money towards them, he hastily resumed his pen.

The happy children lost no time in obeying him, half afraid the concert might be over ere they retraced their steps to Ship Street. But no; the singing was still going on as they crept with timid steps through the half-opened door, and for the first time in their lives entered a Catholic chapel.

It was the sweet Benediction hour, and the altar was brilliantly lighted and decked with flowers. The Rosary had been said, and the first hymn was over, but while the priest was robing in the sacristy, the children and congregation were singing another. A kind-looking old man at the end of the chapel, seeing the children were strangers, pointed to a seat, and gave them a book opened at the hymn at that moment being sung, and as each of our little friends had a good ear for music, they quickly caught up the tune, and were soon singing, with the rest, of that Paradise,

> "Where loyal hearts and true
> Stand ever in the light,
> All rapture through and through,
> In God's most holy sight."

When the hymn was over, came the Benediction, and as the congregation fell on their knees, Effie and Lassie knelt also; and when our Lord Himself looked down upon the neglected children, and blessed them, their angels smiled with unspeakable joy, and gave thanks to God, who had permitted them to guide those little ones into the Presence of His Son. After the priest had closed the door of the tabernacle, the children sang another hymn, which they must have learnt by heart, as the words were not in the book, and of which Effie and Lassie could catch only a few lines.

Long after the congregation had left the church Effie and her sister lingered, as though spell-bound, gazing at the altar; Lassie murmuring softly under her breath, over and over again, the words,

"No, never more! no, never more!"

At last the old sacristan, who had lent them the hymn book, came up and whispered to the awe-stricken children that he was obliged to go away for a while, and must close the church. They rose and followed him into the porch, where Effie timidly held out the shilling her father had given her for the supposed concert.

"What is this for, my child?" inquired the old man in surprise.

"Oh, please sir, I'm afraid it's not half enough for the beautiful sight; but it's all we have, and we could not ask before we came in how much there was to pay, as the door was open, and no one was there."

"Oh!" the old man replied, with a kindly smile, "there is nothing to pay here, my children; the door is always open, except when I go home to meals, or to attend at the cemetery. So you can come every day at the same time if you have a mind, and you will always be very welcome."

"Oh, thank you, sir!" Lassie gratefully replied, while she gazed up into the old man's face with one of her angelic smiles; "we will come every day, if father and mother will give us leave, and I do so hope they will."

"Are your parents Catholics?" inquired the old sacristan, with a somewhat puzzled expression.

"Oh no, sir," replied Effie, without a moment's hesitation; "father was a railway clerk at Balcombe before the accident on the line, and mother is a needlewoman, and makes such beautiful clothes for little ladies and gentlemen."

The old man sighed deeply, well knowing that a Catholic child would have given a very different answer; but having no time to linger, he bade the children good-bye, once more reminding them that the church was open every day till four o'clock, and that they would be always very welcome within its walls.

The happy children hurried home, where they gave so bewildering a description of what they had seen that the mother imagined the chapel was some sort of a school where poor children were taught to sing without any payment, and gladly gave her consent to their attendance when the weather would allow. Indeed, Mrs. Greenwood was only too thankful for the ray of sunshine thus brightening her poor children's otherwise dull and depressing existence, and the father silently acquiesced in the arrangement.

And so it came to pass that Lassie and Effie became frequent visitors at Our Lady's Chapel, and were no longer dull and lonesome as of old, for they were learning to know and to love God in His holy Church; and everything around them became, as it were, tinged and illuminated with its beauty. But, sad to say, neither the children themselves, nor their old friend the sacristan, were conscious that poor Lassie had never been received into its blessed fold, for in consequence of some careless words dropped by Mrs. Greenwood, when speaking jestingly of the old nurse who had taken Effie to be baptized, she had conveyed to their minds the impression that Lassie also had been indebted in like manner to the same good soul; and seldom did the children lie down to sleep without invoking the blessing of God and of our Lady upon the head of their kind though unknown friend.

## CHAPTER III.

### THE WOLF.

The spring had passed quietly away, and summer, her brief life also ended, had died a peaceful death in the arms of golden autumn, which, reserving her brightest flowers to deck the altar on All Saints' Day in honour of the "great multitude that no man can number," had likewise gone to rest. The children of the Church had chanted a *requiem* over their beloved dead, and thousands of Masses had been offered up for the repose of those who sleep in Jesus. The harvest had long since been garnered in the now desolate country; the swallow had flown to brighter climes; and the children in the old house were having a weary time of it, for winter had set in with more than ordinary severity, enveloping the great city in a shroud of snow and fog, making it dangerous for Lassie and Effie to thread their way on Christmas Day through the murky streets to Our Lady's Chapel in Ship Street, where, by the side of the manger, they would gladly have lingered for hours.

Twice or thrice in the course of the summer their mother had taken them by the underground railway to the Kensington Gardens, where she sat at needlework as they ran about under the trees and made merry. They called these little expeditions "going into the country," and enjoyed themselves as only the children of the poor can enjoy their rare, brief holidays.

Mrs. Greenwood was a clever seamstress, and worked for a juvenile establishment at the west-end of London, and the children often gazed with wonder and envy at the delicate white garments she sent away, thinking all the while that the wearers of such fine clothes must be exceptionally happy creatures. Lassie especially used to mingle them in her day-dreams with the Angels of whom she had heard so much in our Lady's Chapel. But it was no easy task now for the anxious father, in that dimly-lighted old room, to decipher the closely-written manuscripts he had to copy; and as from time to time he pressed his hand to his side, or, flinging down his pen, paced up and down the room with an impatient frown, it was plainly evident that he was heart-sick of the ceaseless struggle he had to endure. Finally, too, Mrs. Greenwood's delicate work came to a standstill in consequence of her employer's bankruptcy; and the shop-work which she succeeded in obtaining scarcely paid for the trouble of bringing it from the distant city warehouse where it was given out. Have our young readers ever heard the pathetic "Song of the Shirt?" And do they remember the following verse?

> "Work, work, work,
>   Till the brain begins to swim.
> Work, work, work,
>   Till the eyes are heavy and dim.
> Band and gusset and seam,
> Seam and gusset and band,
> Till over the buttons I fall asleep
> And sew them on in a dream."

Such was Mrs. Greenwood's life, as she sat beside her husband in those dark wintry days, stitching away by the glimmer of a solitary light in that gloomy old room. Dismal work was it indeed for the poor children, whispering together in the corner for hours, in the long evenings ere bed-time arrived; and yet they did not look unhappy, for they seemed to have inexhaustible topics of conversation. Let us for a few moments turn listeners, and hear what they are conversing about so earnestly this evening.

"Don't you wish, Effie," Lassie asked, "that you could see your Guardian Angel? I do so long to see mine, with his beautiful and shining face, and I should like to hear him speak, too; I wonder what his voice is like?"

"Well, do you know," replied Effie, with a thoughtful expression, "I don't think I should like to see my Angel's face before I die."

"Oh!" cried the other child in surprise, "How very strange of you, Effie! Why not?"

"Because," sighed Effie, "I am afraid it might make me feel discontented; and that would never do."

"Discontented!" echoed Lassie; "would you feel discontented at seeing your dear Angel's face? For my part, it would make me feel certain sure that

I *have* a Guardian Angel, if I could only see him sometimes."

"Oh, as to that," was the reply, "I am quite as sure of it as if I really did see him; but I have a sort of feeling that if I were really and truly to look upon his beautiful face I should no longer be happy in this world; I should so long to fly away with him, far, far beyond the sun and moon and stars, and never come back any more to this dark, gloomy old house."

"But," said Lassie, with a troubled look, "you would take me with you? You would not fly away with your Angel, if you could, and leave me behind?"

"Oh, no, no," smiled Effie, clasping her arms round the little one, "I could not bear to do that. But, then, I'm afraid,"—and she paused.

"What are you afraid of, Effie, dear?"

"Why, the worst of it is this," and here followed a deep-drawn sigh from

Effie, "that perhaps my Angel might not be able to carry us both at once to heaven. His wings might not be strong enough; and besides,"—as if a sudden thought had decided the question,—" Father Alban told us that every baptized child has its own special Angel Guardian to watch over it on earth, and carry it up to see God afterwards. So it would be quite impossible, you see, for my Angel to—." Here she was interrupted by a burst of tears from Lassie.

"Why, what is the matter? What have I said to make you cry, pet?" said Effie, kneeling down by the side of the sobbing child.

But no answer came for several moments. Then, with a more than usually beseeching look in her innocent blue eyes, Lassie whispered, "To see God. You said the Angel would take us up to see God. Oh, Effie, I do so long to see Him!"

"But," answered the sister, in an awe-struck voice, "we cannot see God and live."

"Then," sobbed out the child, "I would like to die, for I do so long to see Him! It made such a pain come here, Effie, when you said those words;" and she pressed her little hand to her forehead.

At that moment a large cinder fell from the fast dying fire; and Samuel Greenwood, whose pen had been busily gliding over the paper the last four hours without any intermission, gave a deep groan, and fell back in his chair. He had been subject of late to sudden attacks of faintness, and this was one of them. His wife sprang from her needlework to his side, and the terrified children rushed across the room to assist her.

"Brandy, brandy," gasped the poor sufferer.

"There is not a drop in the house, but I will get some," said Mrs. Greenwood, more frightened than she cared to let the children know.  Here, Effie, dear, hold father's head up till I return; and you, Lassie, rub his hands."  She ran quickly from the room, feeling that her husband's life depended on her haste.

At the foot of the staircase stood a young and gaily-dressed girl, who lived in the same house, and with whom Mrs. Greenwood had a slight acquaintance. "Oh, Maggie," cried the anxious wife, "would you be so kind as to run to the 'Swan' for a little brandy?  My husband is very ill, and I really ought not to leave him."

"Certainly, Mrs. Greenwood," answered the girl; "but there is no need to run to the 'Swan' for the brandy; there is some in my room: I am seldom without it," she added, in a reckless voice, as, springing up the stairs, she returned with a small bottle about half full, and hastened with Mrs. Greenwood to the sick man's side, as though anxious to be of further service.

The sight of the pale children, trying in vain to revive the apparently dying father, brought tears into Maggie's soft dark eyes; but brushing them hastily away, she poured out some brandy, and helped the trembling wife to force it down the sick man's throat.

Mr. Greenwood was fortunately a sober man, and the brandy, in consequence, brought him to himself all the sooner. After a few gasps and deep-drawn sighs, the spasm which had so suddenly overtaken him passed away, and drawing Lassie to his lap, while he folded his arm round the other terrified child, he assured them that "father was all right again," and kissing each little white face with much affection, told them to trot off to bed, as he must go to work again at the papers.

"Not to-night, dear," objected his

wife; "surely not to-night, when you so sadly need rest."

"I must finish them to-night, and let the clerks at the office have them the first thing to-morrow morning, or I shall get no more; they grumbled the other day because the work was behindhand, and what would become of us were I to lose it altogether? It is a hard business, anyhow, to keep the wolf from the door."

"The wolf, father?" whispered Lassie, beginning once more to tremble; "what wolf?"

"Oh, the wolf, my child," replied the father, sadly, "that prowls about a poor man's threshold night and day. Only once let him get his black feet over the door, and there's small chance of escape for those inside."

"Oh, the cruel creature!" shivered Lassie; "it has not been at our door, has it, father?"

"No, but very near it, I fear," replied Mr. Greenwood, rather amused at

Lassie's literal interpretation of his words. "But he shan't get in to hurt my darlings; so run off to bed, and we will see what can be done to keep the naughty wolf out."

Lassie obeyed, holding her sister tightly by the hand, and crept beneath a curtain, behind which an old-fashioned sort of alcove formed a tiny bedroom for the children. But once in bed, her first question, as she clung trembling into Effie's arms, was whether she thought father would be able to keep the horrid creature out.

"I don't know," whispered Effie, "whether father will be able to keep it out; but I know some one else who will never let it come near us."

"Who is that?" sobbed Lassie, the excitement of the last hour having been too much for her.

"Why, the Good Shepherd, of course," said Effie, in a tender, coaxing tone. "Don't you remember what Father

Alban told the school children on Sunday? But that must have been the day you had the headache and fell asleep. Well, he told them that the Good Shepherd who minds the sheep takes particular care of the lambs, because they are more helpless, and He will never let the cruel wolf come near to hurt them. So of course He won't let it come here to hurt us, because we are His lambs."

"Oh, I am so glad we belong to that Good Shepherd," sighed Lassie, laying her head peacefully on the pillow. I will tell father about Him to-morrow; and poor Maggie, too, she looks so lonesome, and has such a pretty face. I hope she belongs to that Shepherd, and then the cruel wolf will never catch her. I should not like the wolf to catch poor Maggie."

In another minute the two children were fast asleep.

## CHAPTER IV.

### LASSIE'S FRIEND.

The next morning, when Mr. Greenwood, who, after a few hours' sleep seemed much as usual, took the papers to the office in the city from which he had procured them, the manager complained of the writing, saying it was not half as good as usual, and that the firm could not afford to have their work copied in that careless manner: and on poor Mr. Greenwood's excusing himself on the score of sickness, the manager smiled scornfully. He was a hard man, with little compassion for others, and too much accustomed to put the worst construction on their actions; so, jumping immediately at the conclusion that poor Mr. Greenwood's hand-shaking was caused by drink, he put down the small sum due to him for the copying, and, saying that he could find hundreds of others who would do the work better, dismissed him altogether from his employment.

Could the manager have seen the look of despair with which the poor fellow left the office he might have given him another trial; but being more than usually busy that morning, he turned to other matters, and was quickly absorbed in them, while the man whom he had so carelessly dismissed made his way home with an aching heart, stopping on his way at a dispensary, to speak to one of the doctors, whom he had lately been forced to consult about his failing health.

Lassie was alone when her father returned, Effie having gone with her mother to help to carry the work to the city. She was busily engaged playing with her doll. She ran eagerly up to him. "Oh, father, I have been showing

Dusy the picture of Red Riding Hood and the wolf that ate the poor little creature up. Look at the horrid thing! Is it like the one you are afraid of, papa dear? Are you still frightened about him?" But receiving no answer, the child climbed up to his knee, and laid her little head fondly on his shoulder.

There is an old saying to the effect that "it is the last straw which breaks the camel's back," and Lassie's silent caress appeared to be the "last straw" in this instance. The poor worn-out father was faint from want of food, and his abrupt dismissal from the office had shaken him terribly; so it was no wonder that at the child's last question his self-control gave way altogether, and, laying his head down on her golden hair, he burst into a passion of tears, such as men seldom shed.

Lassie had never in the course of her short life seen anything like this, and from sympathy, not unmixed with fear, she began to sob also, but on second thoughts resolved to turn comforter; and being firmly convinced that fear of the terrible wolf was at the bottom of this extraordinary burst of grief, she began to wipe away her father's tears, whispering in his ear at the same time, "Don't cry any more, papa dear; I've a secret to tell you; I know how to keep it out. Just listen to me and leave off crying."

Half ashamed of having given way to tears before his little girl, Mr. Greenwood quickly recovered himself, and making an attempt to smile, patted Lassie's head, bidding her lose no time in imparting to him the wonderful secret.

"It is about the wolf," replied the little girl, confidentially; "*I* know how to keep the wicked creature out."

"That's more than I do, then," said her father, unable to repress a smile; "and how is it to be done, then?"

But Lassie was in no hurry, apparently, to supply the information; she wished to know first by what method father had hitherto excluded the animal, and the reason why he was so fearful he could do so no more.

"Why you see, my Lassie," said Mr. Greenwood, keeping up the joke, "since you are so bent upon knowing all about it, my way of keeping the wolf outside the door was by writing those papers; but now the gentleman at the office won't give me any more."

"What, father, dear!" was the astonished answer, "keep the wolf out by writing papers! how very funny! But I suppose," added Lassie, after a few moments' grave consideration, "the horrid creature is afraid of paper, just as a mad bull is of a red cloak. How cruel of those gentlemen not to give you any more of those papers to write! But never mind, papa dear, because I can get some more for you, if you like."

"Well, you are a wonderful little girl, no mistake," laughed her father; "why, I'm half afraid you must be a witch. And pray where does my little Lassie expect to get the papers for father, that are to frighten the wolf from the door?"

"Ah," replied the child, with one of those strange smiles that for some reason or other always gave her father the heart-ache, "I have got a Friend who gives me everything I ask Him for."

"Do you mean down at the school to which you and Effie are so fond of going?"

"Yes, that is the place He lives in," said the little girl, softly, "and He is sure to send you some more papers if I ask Him; so please let Maggie take me down to Ship Street, as Effie is away. I know she will take care of me, because she is such a nice kind girl."

"Oh, is that the name of the young girl who gave mother the brandy for me last night?" asked Mr. Greenwood. "She ran away so quickly afterwards that I had not an opportunity to thank her. Yes, you may go along with her, and be sure to tell her that her brandy saved my life last night, and that I do not forget her kindness. I will lie down a bit while you are away, for my head feels very queer. Be sure to tell your friend in Ship Street that I will do any writing he can give me very reasonably, and be thankful for it."

"Good-bye, papa dear, and don't be unhappy any more, because He is sure, certain sure, to give me what I ask Him for." And Lassie ran for her little cloak and bonnet, and in another minute was on her way with good-natured Maggie to Ship Street.

When they reached the chapel door, Maggie stopped, as if afraid to enter, and telling Lassie she would wait for her on the opposite side of the way, the girl rushed across the muddy road as though some enemy were pursuing her.

Lassie found the chapel empty, so she crept into her usual seat at the rear of the church, and then, suddenly, as though some voice bade her draw nearer, she walked timidly up to the very altar-rails, where, kneeling down and clasping her little hands together, she offered her petition to the "Friend" of whom she had spoken with such confidence and affection to her father.

Lassie's prayer was a very brief one, but it was one of those prayers to which come speedy answers, as so many beautiful stories in Scripture and the Lives of the Saints remind us.

When Lassie's simple prayer was over, she glided round the church, stopping to kiss the images of our Lady and St. Joseph on the way.

The old sacristan—who, unseen, had been watching her with much interest—met her in the porch, and taking her hand, asked her in a kindly tone of surprise how she came to be alone, and what had become of her sister?

"Oh, I'm not alone, thank you, sir," answered Lassie. "Effie has gone with mother to the city, and Maggie brought me down to the chapel, but she wouldn't come in; she is waiting for me over the way."

"Do you mean that young girl across the street?" said the old sacristan, shaking his head, and pointing at poor Maggie, whom he had seen enter a public-house at the end of the street, and return from it looking flushed and excited.

"Yes, that is dear Maggie," was the child's affectionate answer. "She is such a dear girl! She saved father's life last night."

"Has your father been ill?" inquired Mr. Goodman.

"Oh, yes, sir, he was very ill last night, but he is better to-day. He cried this afternoon, and he says it is all about that horrid wolf, because he's afraid he can't keep it out much longer if he does not get some more writing to do; and the gentleman at the office was angry because poor father's hand shakes when he is tired, and they won't give him any more, and so I came down here with Maggie to ask Him" (here the child turned and pointed reverently towards the altar) "to send some more work to father, and then the wolf won't trouble him."

The old sacristan might well be astonished at this extraordinary language, and guessing that something was amiss in Lassie's home, and feeling a great interest in all that concerned her, he asked her a few questions, the answers to which made the story less mysterious.

"And so," said Mr. Goodman, when he saw how matters stood, "you came here to pray for your father, because you are so afraid of the wolf he talks about, did you?"

"Oh, no, sir!" said Lassie; "Effie and I are not one bit afraid of it now, even if it does get into the room, because Effie heard Father Alban say that we were the lambs of the Good Shepherd, and that He never lets the wolf hurt His lambs, because they are so little and so helpless."

The old man was silent for a short time, then he said to her kindly, "Quite right, little one; He never will."

"And do you think He will send father the work before very long?" asked the child.

"I do," was the emphatic reply. "I think He will send it very soon. But here comes your sister, and I am glad of it," said Lassie's friend, looking doubtfully across the road at poor Maggie, who, it must be confessed, did not seem in a fit condition to take care of any one. On seeing Effie join her sister, she nodded a good-bye to the children, and calling out in an incoherent voice that she would be at the house long before they were, hurried away.

After a few moments further conversation with the children, Mr. Goodman bade them good evening, telling them to hurry home, as it was getting late. He stood looking after them, buried in thought, but suddenly, as if inspired by an anxious idea, hurried back into the sacristy, and returning with his hat and stick, locked up the church, and then walked off at an unusually rapid pace in a direction opposite to that taken by his little friends.

No one who met old Mr. Goodman that night, with his hat drawn down over his eyes, and his coat collar turned up to keep out the cold, hesitating when he came to a crossing before he attempted to go over, and pushed and jostled by the busy crowd, would have taken him to be the messenger of a great king. And yet the King of Angels had, in reply to a little child's petition, sent him that very evening on an errand of mercy, and in the good old man's errand was conveyed the answer to Lassie's prayer.

## CHAPTER V.

### THE INVITATION.

When the children reached home, after parting with Mr. Goodman, they were surprised to see Maggie talking to an old woman, whose loud, harsh tones reached their ears as they entered the hall. "You are a downright foolish girl not to come to the theatre with me to-night!" were the first words the children heard. "There's a jolly piece on, with three murders in it, and a suicide, and no end of a ballet afterwards, and songs to cheer one up, after the tragedy."

"Thank you, Mother Darkman," said Maggie, "but I'm quite sick of theatres for the last week or two; they make my head ache, and, to tell you the truth, I can't afford the money, for times are hard just now, and work is scarce."

"Oh!" said the old woman, coaxingly, "I hate to see a young woman like you moping over needlework and spoiling her eyes trying to earn a few shillings. Come along, and we'll have a pleasant night of it."

The girl hesitated, but finally, with a reckless care-for-nothing air, sad to witness in one so young, was about to accept the invitation, when an old organ-grinder, who for some time past had been torturing people's ears with jigs and polkas distractingly out of time, suddenly changed the stop, and struck into the air, "Come back to Erin, mavourneen, mavourneen." The organ was dismally out of tune, and the beautiful melody completely ruined in consequence, but it produced a singular effect upon Maggie. She sprang back from the old woman's side, stamped her foot passionately on the floor, and snatching some coppers from her pocket, hurled them on the ground, exclaiming vehemently, "Give the man that money, and bid him begone, or he will drive me mad."

"Hoity toity! what's the matter now?" said the old woman; "what do you snap at me in this fashion for?"

"Send him away! send him away!" shrieked Maggie, holding her ears with both hands, as if to shut out the sound of the air that had so strangely moved her. "Send him away,—the organ man, I tell you, old woman, or he will drive me mad. I don't want the theatre; I don't want anything. You are an old wolf, and you have just driven me wild with your nonsense." And the excited girl turned and fled up the stairs.

The old woman picked up the money, and looked after Maggie, muttering some unintelligible words.

The terrified children, cowering at the

foot of the staircase, caught the expression of her face as she gazed at poor Maggie's retreating figure, and clung tremblingly to each other.

"Old wolf, indeed!" she muttered, shaking her withered hand in the air; "but I'll be even with her: I'll have my revenge, no fear of that, Miss Maggie. But I'll drink your health first with the money," hissed Mother Darkman, putting the half-pence in her pocket. "Did you think Mother Darkman was such a fool as to give it to that old idiot out there, with his dismal music that's enough to scare a night owl?" And once more shaking her stick after Maggie, she hobbled away down the street.

"Oh, the wicked, wicked old woman," whispered Effie, "to steal poor Maggie's money, and call her such bad names."

But never a word spoke Lassie; springing up the stairs, she darted into her father's presence with flushed cheek and open mouth. She was so unlike his usually quiet, sedate little girl, that Mr. Greenwood looked up astonished.

"Oh, father, father," exclaimed the excited child, scarcely able to bring the words out fast enough, "*I've seen the wolf! I've seen the wolf!* It's dressed up in an old woman's clothes, like the picture in Red Riding Hood, and it's got shaggy hair, and fierce black eyes, just like that wolf has; and it stole poor Maggie's money, and it's going to be revenged upon her, because she wouldn't go along with it. And oh, father, and oh, mother," continued the excited child, "do let me go and warn poor Maggie against it, and tell her to lock her door in case the horrid creature should try to get in." Here the overwrought little maiden burst into a flood of tears, and threw her arms around her mother's neck.

"Why, Effie," said Mr. Greenwood, turning to the other child, who looked almost as bewildered as her sister, "what is all this about? and who has dared to frighten Lassie in this manner?"

"Why, father," explained Effie, "it's all the fault of that old woman they call Mother Darkman; she quarrelled with Maggie because she wouldn't go with her to the theatre; and oh, father, she cursed and swore in such a dreadful manner after Maggie ran away from her."

"Oh, it's that old witch, is it?" replied Mr. Greenwood, with a frown of displeasure; "her curses count for nothing. I'm sorry that girl has anything to say to her, but am glad to hear they've fallen out. Maggie seems to be a good-hearted girl, from all accounts."

"And so she is, father dear," exclaimed Lassie from her mother's knee; "and you and mother will let me go and warn her against the wolf, won't you?"

"Yes, yes, my pet; you and Effie shall go to her after you have had your tea and are quiet again," said Mrs. Greenwood, fondly; " and you may ask her to come and see us sometimes, if father has no objection. She was very kind to us last night, and perhaps we might keep the poor thing out of harm's way," added the wife, looking across to her husband. Mr. Greenwood gladly acquiesced in his wife's suggestion.

So after tea the two children set out hand in hand for Maggie's room, situated at the further end of a long corridor. The moon shone brightly through the old-fashioned oriel window at the end of the passage, and made it luminous as they proceeded. On arriving at Maggie's door a whispered consultation took place as to who should first enter, and it was finally decided that Effie should remain outside and say her Rosary, in order to keep off the *wolf*, while Lassie should venture in and warn Maggie against her enemy.

On the child's entrance, however, no

Maggie was visible. The fire was quite out, and the whole room perfectly dark, except for the moonbeams stealing through the window. After looking about in every direction, Lassie timidly advanced towards an old sofa in one corner of the chamber, upon which Maggie lay, apparently fast asleep; but on Lassie's softly repeating her name, she started up with a stifled scream, and clasping her hands together, while large drops of perspiration stood out on her forehead, she besought the child in piteous accents,—calling her by the name of Minnie, her little sister,—to go back to heaven, and not come there to reproach her.

It was touching to hear her, and had not Lassie's anxiety with regard to the *wolf* overcome for the moment every other feeling, she would in all probability have run away; but the child, young and timid though she was, seemed to be endowed with a courage which the sight of sorrow and suffering never fails to arouse in some souls, however young.

She drew nearer to Maggie, telling her not to be afraid, as it was only Lassie, who had come to speak to her, and begged her to listen to what she had to say.

"O! Lassie, Lassie, how you have scared me!" sobbed the poor girl, rising from the sofa, and sinking wearily into a chair, while she wiped the moisture from her brow; "you—you—looked so like her, my poor little Minnie, my little sister, standing there in the moonlight with your golden hair; and your voice, too, sounded just like hers. But oh! she's dead, and I shall never see her again,—never, never!"

"O, yes you will, Maggie dear," whispered Lassie; "you're sure to see her again if you're good,—up there, you know, among the Angels. I shouldn't wonder," continued the little comforter, "if she were near you now, as near as I am, only you can't see her."

"I hope not," rejoined the girl, almost fiercely. "I don't want her to see me now; it would break her little heart, she loved me so." And Maggie covered her face with her hands, while the tears streamed between her tightly clasped fingers.

Lassie stood by in silence, wholly at a loss what to do or say; but silence is oftentimes more eloquent than words, and Maggie seemed soothed by this mute sympathy; for, after a while, becoming calmer, she looked up and asked Lassie whether father was ill again, or anything the matter at home.

"Oh, no," answered the little girl, much relieved by Maggie's question; "father is all right again, but he and mother have given me leave to come and warn you against the *wolf*, and tell you to be sure and lock your door lest he should get in; and Effie is saying her Rosary outside to keep it off."

"The wolf, child!" echoed Maggie; "is everybody foolish to-night, I wonder, as well as I am? What in the name of all that's good do you mean?"

"I'm not foolish a bit," answered Lassie, smiling; "but you must listen to what I say, or it will do you harm, for it has stolen your money, and looked so spiteful at you; and it has vowed to be revenged because you were so angry with it. But perhaps you never read the story of Red Riding Hood, and don't know that a wolf can dress up like an old woman; but," continued Lassie, drawing up her small figure with amusing dignity, "I know all about it, so that's the reason I came to warn you."

"Well, I declare!" cried Maggie, her sorrow suddenly changing into a dreary sort of mirth: "why, it must be old Mother Darkman the child means. Oh, my!" and she rocked herself to and fro, and laughed till the tears ran down her cheeks, and then sobbed, and then laughed again, till poor Lassie was quite alarmed, and begged her to leave off.

"You see," argued the child, with much solemnity, " it really is nothing to laugh at."

"You're right there, little one," gasped Maggie, making a desperate effort at self-control; "there's nothing to laugh at in Mother Darkman; she's an old wolf and no mistake, and the worst wolf that ever I met; and mind," she exclaimed, springing to her feet, "mind that neither you nor your sister ever go near her, or she'll do you harm some of these days, you poor little innocent creatures."

"Oh, never mind us," laughed Lassie, triumphantly; "it can't hurt us, you know, because we belong to One who won't let it; and if you'll only do what I want you to, Maggie dear," she added, in a coaxing tone, "it won't be able to hurt you either."

"And pray, who may that be, my dear?" inquired the girl, upon whose mind Lassie's earnest manner was making an impression.

"Why, I want you," pleaded Lassie, "to come down with me on my birthday to Our Lady's Chapel, and speak to the Good Shepherd, who lives there, about the horrid wolf, and ask Him not to let it hurt you. It is so beautiful down there. There is a picture, too, in one part of the church, which reminds Effie and I of you; she's got a face just like yours,—the girl who is kneeling there, I mean,—and she is kissing the feet of the Good Shepherd, and washing them with her tears,—because she has been naughty, I suppose, and is very sorry. He is looking down at her with such a look; I can't tell you what it's like; come down, please, and see it with me."

"Stop, stop, Lassie!" sobbed Maggie, laying her head down on the table; "I can't bear it any longer. "Oh dear, what shall I do? what *shall* I do?"

"Why, do what I ask you to do," said the child, putting her little arms round the girl's waist; "come down there with me on my birthday, and you'll soon be happy. It's the day after tomorrow, the Feast of the Holy Innocents; and father and mother have promised to do anything I ask them when it comes, because they are too poor to give me a present; so I have made up my mind to ask them to come down there with me on my birthday morning. They must come, or else they would break their promise; and so do, dear Maggie, go with us, and then we can all come back to tea together, and have such a happy evening, for I mean to invite old Mr. Goodman. Mother is going to make a cake, and we will have games afterwards. It will be such a happy birthday. So you will come, won't you?"

"I will see about it, dear Lassie," said Maggie, bending towards the child; "and I thank you very much for asking me. No, no," she exclaimed, as the child put up her rosebud lips for a kiss, "no, no, Lassie dear, I cannot kiss you, I am not good enough; but," she added, as the child, with a look of disappointment, went towards the door in obedience to Effie's call, who peeped in to say it was time to return, "when you meet my little sister in heaven, Lassie, as you will some day, she will kiss you instead."

Softly closing the door after the two children, Maggie returned to her poor bed, where, throwing herself on her knees, she sobbed for hours, while good and evil Angels fought an unseen fight beside her, and struggled hard for the mastery over her half-despairing soul. Which of the two will conquer? That depends on Maggie herself; she, and she alone, can and must choose between them.

## CHAPTER VI.

### THE KING'S MESSENGER.

At a late hour on the afternoon following the children's visit to Maggie's room, as Mr. Greenwood was sitting alone, perusing with anxious eyes the advertisements in some daily papers, hoping to discover in their columns something that would suit his necessities, he was surprised by a knock at the door. On opening it he found himself face to face with a benevolent-looking old gentleman, who apologized for his intrusion by saying that he was acquainted with Mr. Greenwood's little girls, and having learned from the younger child that her father was in want of employment, he had called to tell him of a situation that he thought would be acceptable.

Mr. Greenwood begged the gentleman to be seated, and on hearing that the situation so unexpectedly offered to him was that of confidential clerk to a house of business in the city, the duties of which he was fully competent to undertake, tears of joy and gratitude rose to his eyes.

The old gentleman went on to explain that it would be necessary for Mr. Greenwood to be at his post by nine o'clock each morning, but that, as an omnibus passed the corner of the adjoining street every half hour, he trusted there would be no difficulty on that score.

"No difficulty!" exclaimed the grateful listener; "why, sir, it will be the saving of my life; the fresh air going to and from the city is the very thing I need. The doctor told me only this morning that if I did not get more air he would not answer for the consequences. Oh, sir," he cried, rising impulsively, and holding out his hand to the old sacristan, for it was he, "how can I ever thank you enough for your kindness? And only to think," he continued, "that my brave little girl should really have had the sense to go and tell you all about my troubles. Why, to tell you the truth, sir, I almost fancied it was some imaginary friend my Lassie was talking about, for she often seems to be in a sort of dream, away up in the clouds, as the saying is."

"She does, indeed," was the old man's reply; "she is a strangely thoughtful child for one so young. But," he continued, smilingly, "you are mistaken, Mr. Greenwood, in supposing that I was the friend whom your little girl sought out so eagerly on your account last evening. It was only by the merest accident that I came to hear of your loss of employment, otherwise I could perhaps have been of service to you before."

"Then," inquired the father, in much

surprise, "who could it have been? I am more puzzled than ever."

The old man made no reply, but stood thoughtful, and for some moments looked on the ground; then raising his eyes to Mr. Greenwood's face, he asked whether he would give him permission, before answering his question, to put one to him.

"Certainly, sir," was the courteous reply; "you are at liberty to ask me any questions that may seem good to you."

"Then," said the old man quickly, and as though afraid of hurting his listener's feelings, "I am anxious for many reasons to learn, Mr. Greenwood, whether you are a Catholic or not; it is from no motive of idle curiosity, believe me, that I venture to ask this question."

It was now Mr. Greenwood's turn to remain silent, and for some minutes Mr. Goodman feared that Lassie's father was offended. Such, however, was not the case; Mr. Greenwood was not a man given to take offence where none was intended, and there was something in the old sacristan's manner that appealed to the best feelings of his heart, which, though a careless, had never been a hard one. After an embarrassing pause, therefore, he replied in a low tone, as though half ashamed of his words, "I hardly know how to answer your question, sir. I was a Catholic thirty years ago, and I have no faith in any other religion, but,"—and again he became silent.

"I see, I see," said the old man, in a tone of sorrow. "For thirty years, poor soul, you have, like too many others, turned your back upon your best Friend, and He,—ah, it is the old, old story,—He has not forsaken you in your hour of trouble."

There was no reply. The Angel Watcher, who had so long stood by Samuel Greenwood's side, with that stern expression on his face, drew near. Oh, how long and how patiently had the good Angel waited for this hour, another hour of grace granted in answer to the earnest and ceaseless prayer for the soul committed to his charge!

At length the old sacristan asked Mr. Greenwood, in a kind and gentle tone, whether he had his leave to say more.

"Most certainly, my kind friend," was the answer; "you are at perfect liberty to say what you please; you have done me a favour which I shall not forget till my dying day. Go on, sir, go on. And so it was not you, after all, to whom my dear little Lassie applied to obtain me some employment, or what she calls," said the fond father, with a smile, "help to enable me to keep the wolf from the door? Would you believe, sir," he continued, "that she really thinks it was a real wolf I spoke of the other evening when I feared things were going wrong with me, and I happened to use that expression? But pray, sir, do not keep me any longer in ignorance of the other kind friend besides yourself, to whom I am so deeply indebted."

The old sacristan tried to reply, but some inward emotion prevented him. At length, however, in a half-smothered voice, he turned his eyes to heaven, and said, with much reverence, "It was the Friend, Mr. Greenwood, whom for thirty years, according to your own admission, you have turned your back upon."

Sudden and unbidden tears rose to Mr. Greenwood's eyes at the old man's strange reply. Of what was he thinking as he stood gazing out so steadfastly at the darkness? The short winter's afternoon is over, and the stars, those "forget-me-nots of the Angels," appear one by one, "making the night holy." Does its beauty steal into the father's weary soul, recalling to his memory nights,—oh, so long ago!—when he knelt, a happy, innocent child at his mother's knee, and lisped his evening prayer? Does the long-forgotten "Hail Mary" rise almost unconsciously to his lips as he remembers his dear departed mother?

Let us return to our old friend, the "King's Messenger," at the other end of the room. Having delivered his Master's message, he is preparing to depart, saying he has a sick man to call upon in the upper storey of the house, and must therefore say farewell.

"But not without seeing the children," exclaimed Mr. Greenwood, starting from his reverie, and returning to the fireside; "they will be so disappointed on their return not to have seen you, and I expect them and my wife every minute. They must have been caught in one of the heavy showers which you only just escaped; I hope they have found shelter somewhere, as Lassie is so liable to take cold. I conclude," he continued, in a hesitating voice, "from what you told me, that the school I was under the impression my children had been so long attending is in reality a Catholic chapel. Had I not been so absorbed in keeping the wolf from the door I might have guessed it before. And so my little Lassie went down there to pray for me yesterday, did she, and spoke to you afterwards? God bless her for it!" he concluded.

"Yes, and she will be blessed," answered the old man reverently, using the beautiful words of Isaac when blessing his son. "I shall never forget the expression of her eyes," said the old sacristan, "as she raised them towards the tabernacle yesterday. I was in the sacristy, and unseen was watching her the whole time. Mr. Greenwood, you are a fortunate man, in spite of your troubles and anxieties, to possess such a child as Lassie. But may I ask you, bye the bye," continued the old man, "to tell me your little girl's baptismal name, as I am anxious to give her a birthday present to-morrow, and I fancy she would like a book? Lassie is a very pretty pet name, and much used, I believe, in Scotland, so no doubt you have relations there; but I should like to insert my little friend's baptismal name, as well as her pet one, in her birthday present, and I have forgotten to ask her what it is."

A blush of shame rose to Mr. Greenwood's face, but he made no answer.

"Mr. Greenwood," said the old gentleman in a stern voice, for the first time recoiling from the conscience-stricken man before him, "it surely cannot be possible that your children are unbaptized, and you a Catholic, or, at all events, brought up in the Church of Christ! I implore you—"

"No need to implore me, sir," interrupted the father, springing up and pacing the room to and fro with passionate gestures; "I deserve all that you or any one else can say. Effie is baptized, thanks to a stranger,"—and he laid his hand heavily on Mr. Goodman's shoulder,—"but Lassie! O, how soon can I make amends to her! When can she be baptized? Could you arrange it for to-morrow? It is her birthday, and I could take her down to the chapel myself."

"I will speak to Father Alban on my return, and I am certain he will not refuse, as your little girl is so well instructed in her religion. As to her *Faith*,—ah! Mr. Greenwood, if we only had that child's perfect though simple faith, what might we not obtain? But I must leave you now, sorry as I am to go without seeing the children. I will ask Father Alban to call upon you in the morning, and speak to Lassie, who, I fear, will be grieved to hear that with all her love for our Lord she has not yet been admitted into His blessed Fold.

But cheer up, my poor friend," added the kind old man, seeing how deeply Mr. Greenwood was suffering; "all will be set right to-morrow, please God, and then,"—and he gave a searching look into Mr. Greenwood's face.

"No fear of *that*, sir," was the quick reply to the old man's look. "I shall be an altered man from this day; my Lassie's faith has changed my heart."

"To-morrow, then, my friend, we will meet at the Church of Our Lady in Ship Street; it is the Feast of the Holy Innocents."

"Yes; to-morrow, sir," replied the father, returning the old man's earnest hand-shake, while opening the door for his departure; "to-morrow you will see me with Lassie, and I trust you will honour us with your presence afterwards at her little birthday-feast, poor as it will be." And receiving a smiling assent from the old man, Mr. Greenwood closed the door.

"To-morrow," sighed the Angel sentinel, as Lassie's father returned to the hearth, and knelt down beside it. "To-morrow! and who among earth's children can be sure of to-morrow? Human flowers are strangely fragile, and wither oftentimes, ah, so quickly, more quickly than even the flowers by the wayside. What if to-morrow Lassie were no longer here?"

## CHAPTER VII.

### THE RETURN HOME.

An hour or two later in the evening, as Mr. Goodman was descending the staircase, having finished his visit to the sick man in the upper storey of the old house, he was accosted by Maggie, who begged him to excuse the liberty she took in addressing him, and told him in a few simple words of Mr. Greenwood's difficulties, not suspecting that the benevolent old man was aware of them.

Mr. Goodman, greatly pleased at Maggie's change of manner and appearance, and still more so by her anxiety to perform an act of kindness, gave her an account of his visit to Lassie's father, and then inquired, with his usual kindness of manner, whether he could be of any service to herself.

The girl shook her head despondingly, but made no reply.

Mr. Goodman, however, was not easily discouraged when intent on his Master's business, and judging from the girl's accent that she belonged to the Isle of Saints, the dear old Land of Faith, he asked her in a tone of much interest if she was a Catholic.

"I am from Ireland," was the half-inaudible reply, as the large tears rose to her eyes, and coursed down her white cheeks.

"Oh, that is the same thing," answered the old man, cheerily; "blessings on the dear old land that always kept the true faith when other nations fell away from and forsook it. But, my child," he continued, in a still more gentle voice, "you always seem to be alone; have you no friends in London?"

"Not one," was the mournful reply; "not a soul to care for me in this great city, except that dear little child upstairs, whom I would die for," she exclaimed, passionately. "But—but—I am no fit companion for dear little Lassie." And the tears flowed more freely than before.

"My poor child, why are you not at service?" inquired the old man. "A nursemaid's place would be the thing for you, where you could soon make friends of your little charges, and lead a far happier and better life."

"I have no one to recommend me to such a place," was the sad rejoinder. "I have lost my character; I have been in prison. No one would take me, and it is useless for me to try."

"Oh, if that is the case, my poor child," said Mr. Goodman, "I could get you into a convent for a few months, where you might regain your character, and where the good nuns would help you to recover your peace of mind. And indeed something tells me," he added, "that you need only a helping hand to set you in the right path once more. So come down to the chapel to-morrow morning, and I will ask Father Alban to give you a letter of introduction to the Sisters of the Good Shepherd. Meanwhile, pray accept a trifle for your present wants," he added, holding out some money; "you look cold and ill this bitter night."

At that moment a hideous, mocking laugh startled the old sacristan, and turning round he perceived an old woman hobbling towards them from a dark corner beneath the staircase.

"I told you I would have my revenge," she muttered, as she came up to Maggie, hissing the words in the girl's ear; "I told you I would pay you off for your impudence, and so I will." And then changing her tone into one of cringing humility, she courtesied respectfully to Mr. Goodman, and begged him not to waste his money on that girl, as she was sorry to tell him it would only be spent at the gin-shop: the girl to whom he was speaking having been, she was grieved to say, three times in prison for drunkenness. And then, again, as if unable to restrain her spiteful anger, the old wretch shook her wrinkled hand in Maggie's face.

"Begone, woman, and leave the girl alone!" exclaimed the old sacristan, in a tone of disgust and indignation; "or I will place you in charge of the police. I know your character very well; I have seen you before—"

"So have I," muttered a gruff voice behind Mother Darkman, and at the same moment a policeman's hand was laid heavily on her shoulder, and a pair of handcuffs unceremoniously fastened on her wrists. "I fancy you have seen me before, too, old lady, though you have given me the slip for some time back; but I've caught you at last, and you will not escape so easily this time,

I assure you. The charges against you this time are rather serious ones, if I'm not mistaken." And, whistling to another officer who stood at the door, old Mother Darkman was led out of sight.

Maggie watched the terrible old woman's departure with a shudder, and then, turning to Mr. Goodman with an expression piteous to behold, she exclaimed, vehemently: "It is but too true, sir; she has spoken only the truth; I have been three times in prison, and it was there I first met her, and I've been worse and worse ever since."

Just at that moment the door of Mr. Greenwood's room which faced the old staircase was blown open by the wind, which had been rising all the evening, and was now moaning dismally through the house, as though intoning a *Miserere* over the sins of its inhabitants; and the voice of Lassie singing a hymn ere she retired for the night, was wafted on the air. How sweet were the childish tones as she sang:

"O Paradise! O Paradise!
  Wherefore doth death delay?
  Bright death that is the welcome dawn
  Of our eternal day."

Maggie's sobbing ceased, and she listened with upraised head and rapt expression to the hymn, every word of which was distinctly audible. Mr. Goodman looked upward and listened also. How little did either he or Maggie imagine that they were listening to Lassie's last song on earth; how little did they, or any one but the Angels, understand that the "welcome dawn of that eternal day" was about to dawn on the singer; that never again would that bird-like voice sound in "sweet echoes of the songs above" in their ears, unless, by God's mercy, they hear it among the Angels.

Maggie's very soul seemed to shine

through her eyes as she drank in the words of Lassie's unconscious farewell to earth. But when the child reached the fifth verse:

"O Paradise! O Paradise!
I want to sin no more:
I want to be as pure on earth
As on thy spotless shore,"

every word of which fell on Maggie's ear with strange distinctness, the expression of her face underwent an entire change, and clasping her hands together, she exclaimed in a voice that startled the old sacristan: "I do want to sin no more. And oh, my God!" she ejaculated, in tones so earnest that the dark spirit watching her so attentively vanished altogether, "with the assistance of Thy holy grace, I will sin no more!" Then, gathering her shawl about her, the poor lost sheep, so sorely tempted and storm-driven, fled out into the bitter night, but not alone, and no longer in despair, for a radiant figure followed her. And that night there was joy, not only among the Angels in heaven, but also in the Church of our Lady of the Sacred Heart, over another poor sinner who did penance; and long ere the Feast of the Holy Innocents dawned, had laid her down in peace, absolved and forgiven.

## CHAPTER VIII.

Mr. and Mrs. Greenwood sat up late that night, talking over the events of the day, and of the bright future in store for them, thanks to Mr. Goodman's kindness. Mr. Greenwood told his wife of the promise he had given to have Lassie baptized on the following afternoon, and she gladly consented to be present, saying that she had often desired to see the inside of a Catholic church, but had never yet had an opportunity of doing so.

It was shortly after midnight, and they were about to retire, when the sound of distant thunder arrested them, and in another quarter of an hour a severe storm burst over the neighbourhood. The children had gone to rest after singing Lassie's favourite hymn; they were completely worn out, and were also somewhat feverish, having returned home with their mother, soon after Mr. Goodman's departure, completely drenched. After giving them a warm drink and dry clothing, she had sent them off quickly to bed, feeling somewhat anxious about them. They had not heard a word about the arrangement for the following day, and Lassie had sunk to sleep, her little heart brimful of the project she had confided to Maggie, of getting father and mother to the Chapel of Our Lady on her birthday.

How strange and sad that father and child should unconsciously, and at the very same hour, have so arranged a meeting that was never to take place. God willed it otherwise, and He knows best. Lassie was to have her white robe, whiter by far than the robes she dreamed of when playing beneath the trees in the Kensington Gardens. But she is not to win the robe in the Chapel of our Lady, as human hearts had so fondly, but ah! how vainly, arranged for her. Sleep on, dear little Lassie; sleep your last sleep on earth, your last sleep in this world of sin and pain.

Why does Effie's Angel bend over the two little sisters that night with such a strange smile on his radiant brow, half-sad, half-triumphant? Do the Angels weep with those that weep, and rejoice with those who rejoice, as earth's children are bidden to do? If so, they must often, even amid all their joy and their glory, be very sorrowful, for earth's partings are, ah! so bitter, and wounded hearts so hard to heal.

The parents sat listening to the thunder, and watching the lightning flash through the room, wondering whether the tired children would sleep through such a storm, when suddenly they started to their feet, aroused by a sound far more dreary to those loving ears than the moaning storm without. It was a sound to which they were but too well accustomed, the sound of Lassie gasping from a sudden attack of croup, with which she was frequently troubled during the winter months. Two months ago the doctor had warned her mother of the child's extreme delicacy, saying her constitution was too weak to bear any longer the severe remedies which were necessary to subdue that too often fatal complaint of childhood. Notwithstanding this remembrance, the poor mother's first entreaty to her husband as they reached their darling's bedside was, " Run for the doctor;" and in a few moments the doctor's kind face was bending over Lassie, and he was doing his utmost to relieve her sufferings. But alas! his efforts were unavailing; and, having other patients dangerously ill to visit in the course of the next two hours, he was at length obliged to leave, shaking his head sorrowfully, for, like all who knew her, he was attached to Lassie.

"If we could only help her," sobbed Effie, as, standing by the bed with her parents, she watched the terrible convulsions; and suddenly, as though her wish were granted, the spasms ceased, and raising herself convulsively from the pillow, the dying child reached forth her arms to her sister, while the pleading look we have already referred to in our story became more piteously beseeching than ever.

"What is it, darling? what is it, Lassie dear? what do you wish for?" cried Effie, bending eagerly towards her.

"I want,—oh, I want—*to see God!*" gasped the child.

"And so you shall see Him soon, my darling," sobbed Effie.

"Are you sure?" whispered the child, in a faint voice, gazing up into her sister's face.

"Oh, yes, quite sure, darling; all

baptized children see the face of God for ever and ever in heaven, don't they, father dear?" cried Effie, as if anxious for some other voice to approve her words and soothe her sister.

"Oh, my God!" groaned the wretched man; "what have I done! what have I done! *She is not baptized*, Effie; she was to have been. O God of mercy, have pity!"

"Oh, father, father!" sobbed Effie, wringing her hands in passionate sorrow, "run for a priest, run for Father Alban! See, see! the spasms are returning! Oh, hurry, father, or it will be too late!"

Mr. Greenwood staggered to the door, but ere he reached it one of the heart attacks he so often suffered from overcame him, and he sank to the ground. His wife ran to his assistance. The dying child was once more in convulsions, and her sufferings were terrible to witness.

"Oh, Mother of Sorrows! Oh, Mother of Divine Love! She will die unbaptized! Oh, my Lassie! Oh, my own little Lassie!" murmured the poor father.

"Not so," said Effie's Angel-watcher, drawing nearer to the sobbing child, as he reminded her of what she had heard Father Alban say regarding baptism. Leaving the bedside for a moment, she returned with a stoup of holy water, given to the children by the old sacristan, and, bending over her little sister, Effie sprinkled the water on her brow, pronouncing at the same time those blessed words which won for the fluttering soul eternal life: "Lassie, I baptize thee in the name of the Father, and of the Son, and of the Holy Ghost." Thus solemnly, and in trembling tones, were the words pronounced; then, kneeling down, Effie made the sign of the cross on the marble forehead, and softly kissed it.

As the holy water touched the child's

brow the convulsion ceased, and when the sign of the cross she had learned to love so much was imprinted there, a smile of unutterable happiness lit up Lassie's face, while by her side another spirit suddenly appeared, to whom his fellow Angel smiled, as to a beloved and well-known companion. This last comer bore in his right hand a small white robe of dazzling brightness, which he threw around the dying form of the little one. In his left hand he carried a tiny harp and a crown of lilies.

Lassie's dark blue eyes, no longer pleading, but blissful, as though she understood the greatness of the gift that had been bestowed upon her, were raised upward. Then, turning them with a look of tender affection upon the patient, devoted little sister weeping by her side, she stretched out her arms, and gazing up into Effie's face with a look full of joy, the rosebud lips smiled as they had never smiled on earth before, and the dying voice, still full of melody, almost sang the words, " Effie, Effie, I shall at last see God."

In another moment, swifter than the lightning flashing through the room, the little white-robed soul was cradled in the arms of our Lady; another moment it lay on the Heart of Jesus. She did indeed see God,—her yearning was satisfied at last.

## CHAPTER IX.

#### CONCLUSION.

Six years have passed since Lassie died, and now once more, and for the last time, we ask our young readers, ere we bid them farewell, to enter with us the Church of our Lady of the Sacred Heart, in Ship Street. It is again the Feast of the Holy Innocents, and likewise the anniversary of Lassie's threefold birthday: her earthly one, her baptism, and the day on which she awoke to everlasting life.

The feast fell on a Sunday, and there was High Mass in Our Lady's Chapel. It was crowded with worshippers, and thronged, as all Catholic churches are, by unseen and immortal ones. Ah! if we could but see them for a few moments, and observe how they assist at the Holy Sacrifice of the Mass! No wandering looks, no disturbing thoughts, no curiosity as to what others are doing or wearing, troubles these angelic worshippers; with eyes cast downward, or fixed steadfastly on priest and altar, with folded hands, and hearts filled with burning love, they adore their Jesus truly present on His altar.

There are four persons kneeling side by side not far from the altar. They are not strangers to us, though years have made quite a change in their appearance. That white-haired man, whose face is hidden from sight as he listens so attentively to the *Gloria in excelsis*, is the old sacristan; but it is not the dear old sacristan, for he has gone up higher; he adores his God no longer in a temple made with hands. The white-haired figure is Mr. Greenwood. His hair turned perfectly white on that night of agony, six years ago, when Lassie left him for her eternal home. On recovering partially from the spasm which had so unexpectedly seized him that night, he tottered to his child's bedside, imploring his wife to fly to the presbytery in Ship Street, and beg the priest there to come at once and baptize Lassie; but on reaching the bed after Mrs. Greenwood's departure what a sight met the unhappy father's eyes! Two little marble forms lay there, both apparently lifeless, for Effie had fainted away by Lassie's side, and it was many hours before she recovered sufficiently to explain to her father what had taken place; and it was the cruel agony of remorse and self-reproach endured during the hours of Effie's stupor that had silvered his hair and made him prematurely old. But the despair that took possession of Mr. Greenwood's soul that night was changed into the sorrow of true repentance, when on the following morning he heard from the lips of the child that remained to him of Lassie's baptism; and as the father, with broken heart, knelt by the side of the little body covered with snowdrops and primroses, —poor Maggie's birthday gift to Lassie, —Samuel Greenwood made a solemn resolution, that if God in His mercy would only give him time to redeem the past, he would strive to become worthy to meet his Lassie when he should be called to his final account. That vow he has faithfully kept; and as if to prove to the contrite man that his penitence was accepted by God, he had the joy of seeing his wife received into the Church, won over to the true Faith by the good example and fervent prayers of her husband.

As to Effie and Maggie, now fellow-servants in one family, they are more like sisters than friends, and as they kneel there side by side, their Guardian Angels smile fondly at them. Effie Greenwood, though only a servant in a tradesman's family, would not exchange her lot for that of an empress. If we tell our dear young readers that she is one of God's hidden saints, they will perhaps imagine that she neglects her daily duties in order to read holy books or say long prayers, but this is quite a mistake. Her employer has a large family, and she is obliged to work hard from morning till night.

Maggie also is very happy and very peaceful, but her happiness is of an altogether different nature from that of Effie's, as the lot of "those who have sinned, though much they love," must ever be in this world. When I tell you that poor Maggie carries about with her a broken heart, you must not picture her to yourselves as moping round the house with a face as long as her working apron, making every one that looks at her wretched, for we do not believe in all London there were two more cheerful servants than she and Effie. Their master often observes to his wife that it did him good to hear those two girls laughing together in the kitchen, or singing cheerfully as they sat at their needlework in the evening.

But the choir is silent now, and Father Alban is reading the Gospel of the day in English,—reading of "Rachel bewailing her children, and would not be comforted, because they are not." And many a mother as she listens wipes a tear from her eye, remembering how often she too, like Rachel, has refused all consolation because her darlings were taken from her. But when Father Alban begins his sermon, and pictures to his hearers in glowing colours the meeting of Rachel with her little ones, in the Land of Love, tears are changed into smiles. Has the good priest, so beloved by his people, seen the Land of Love he speaks of so fondly? One would almost imagine, to listen to him, that he must have seen it.

Another half hour passes, and High

Mass is over. So we bid farewell to the Church of our Lady, and accompany the old friends we have seen kneeling there together to their home. A long walk lay before them, as Mr. Greenwood and his family no longer lived in the gloomy old house so familiar to our readers, but in the pretty ivy-covered lodge of Kensal Green Cemetery, of which he is now, through Father Alban's influence, the keeper; and it is to this peaceful little home, surrounded by its garden filled with flowers and evergreens, that they now turned their steps.

After a short repast, the whole party, with newly-made wreaths of evergreens and flowers in their hands, strolled together through the cemetery. How peaceful and how beautiful looked those narrow sleeping chambers of our loved ones, decorated by tender hands with wreaths of holly and mistletoe, entwined with immortelles, those flowers which speak so silently to our hearts of the resurrection of the body and the life of the world to come.

> "O Paradise! O Paradise!
> Wherefore doth death delay?
> Bright death that is the welcome dawn
> Of our Eternal day."

How these words re-echoed in the ears of the mourners as they bent their steps towards Lassie's grave! It was her last song on earth, the song which finished the work begun in poor Maggie's wavering soul that night so many years ago, and sent her weeping to the fold which Lassie had been pleading with her to re-enter.

The little child's grave lies at the further end of the cemetery, beneath some old trees, where in summer the birds build their nests, and sing to her the livelong day, and where the lodge-keeper often lingers at night to watch and pray when all is still around—but not for her who sleeps beneath; the

Angels do not need our prayers. A short distance beyond lies another grave, and the inscription on the cross above it tells us that Stephen Goodman is resting there, while the story of the old man's earthly life is recorded in the words beneath:

"Blessed are the merciful,
For they shall obtain mercy."

The mourners poured forth a heartfelt, loving prayer by the grave of their old friend and benefactor, and, hanging a fresh wreath of flowers round the cross, turned to their Lassie's. Are those tears we see stealing down each cheek?—tears still, and Lassie in heaven so many years! Do they want her back again? Would they ask, even could their prayer be granted, to hear her sweet voice again among them, to see her eyes fixed upon theirs from day to day, from year to year, in this land of sorrow and of sin? Would the temptation be too great if set before them? Would they say, "Yes, let her come back"? Not at all. Not for all the wealth and all the joy that earth could yield them. But for all that they must weep on. Tears at least are blameless; nay more, they are among our Father's choicest gifts to His children in this world of woe. In heaven, where tears would be wasted, He Himself will wipe them from all eyes.

One more glance at Lassie's grave, and our story is at an end. A small white cross marks the spot, but the inscription at the foot is so hidden by flowers, even in winter time, that we can with difficulty decipher the words.

✠

**TO THE SWEET MEMORY OF**
## LASSIE,
**WHO DIED ON THE DAY OF HER BAPTISM,**
The Feast of the Holy Innocents, 1868,
**AGED 7 YEARS.**

In the centre of the cross there are three other words, and these are in gilt. These words, so beloved and honoured by Lassie's father, the words whose cadence falls like music on his ears, "like bells at evening pealing," as he looks homeward to his rest; the words which arrest the footsteps of many a sorrowing one passing near the tiny flower-covered grave, and point to the Land where there shall be no more death, are—

"I See God!"

Printed by Richardson and Son, Derby.

**RICHARDSON AND SON'S PUBLICATIONS.**
23, King Edward Street, City, London; and Derby.

*Now Ready, demy 8vo, with* Portrait of the Saint, *superfine cloth, lettered in gold, price 6s.*

## THE LIFE OF
# ST. JOHN BAPTIST DE ROSSI,

Translated from his Biographies,

## BY LADY HERBERT.

### INTRODUCTION:
### ON ECCLESIASTICAL TRAINING AND SACERDOTAL LIFE.
### BY THE BISHOP OF SALFORD.

---

*Demy 8vo, strongly bound in cloth, price* 10s.
### AN ENGLISH EDITION OF
### ORIGINAL, SHORT, AND PRACTICAL
# SERMONS
For every **FEAST** of the Ecclesiastical Year.
#### Three Sermons for every FEAST.
### BY F. X. WENINGER, S.J.,
Doctor of Theology.

☞ This volume is the complement of Father Weninger's "Sunday Sermons," and is bound uniform with them.

---

### BY THE SAME AUTHOR.
*Demy 8vo, strongly bound in cloth, price* 10s., *the*
### SECOND ENGLISH EDITION OF
### ORIGINAL, SHORT, AND PRACTICAL
# SERMONS
For every **SUNDAY** of the Ecclesiastical Year.

Three Sermons for every Sunday.

**RICHARDSON AND SON'S PUBLICATIONS.**
23, King Edward Street, City, London; and Derby.

## NEW SHILLING SERIES OF
# CATHOLIC TALES,
Foolscap 8vo, handsomely bound in Cloth, with black printing on side, and lettered in gold.

**Lassie, and her Guardian Angel.** By Charlotte Dean, authoress of "May Templeton."

**Eva; or, as the Child, so the Woman.** By A. I. O'Neill Daunt.

**The Queen's Confession;** or, the Martyrdom of ST. JOHN NEPOMUCENE. By the Rev. J. J. K., O.S.F.

**Elsie Mc'Dermott,** the Little Watercress Girl. By M. A. Pennell.

**Hilda's Victory;** and Una's Repentance. Tales by M. F. S.

**Little Musicians who became great Masters.** First Series. Translated by Mrs. Townsend.

**Little Musicians who became Great Masters.** Second Series. Together with the FLOWERS of CHILDHOOD. Translated by Mrs. Townsend.

**Ellerton Priory.** A Tale. By the author of "Claire Maitland."

**Little Flower Basket.** By Canon Schmid.

**The Search for Happiness,** and other Tales for Young People.

**Marie, the Fisherman's Daughter.**

**Godfrey, the Little Hermit.** By Canon Schmid.

**The Forest Pony,** the Gipsy Boy, and other Tales, by Lady Elizabeth Douglas.

**The Gift:** containing three interesting Tales.

**Child-Life and its Lessons.** Poetry, Original and Selected.

To be followed by others.

# RICHARDSON AND SON'S PUBLICATIONS.
23, King Edward Street, City, London; and Derby.

Just Published, Demy 18mo, handsomely bound in cloth,

PRICE 6d. EACH.

## CATHOLIC TALES FOR THE YOUNG.

MORNING AND EVENING STAR.
CHRISTMAS DINNER.
HAWTHORN BUSH.
PEARL LOST & FOUND.
THE HOLY HOUSE.
MAURICE'S TRIAL.
CARRY'S TRIALS.

ALTAR FLOWERS.
A TALE OF THE CRUSADERS.
LIFE OF FREDDY WRAGG Br. M. Aloysius, Tertiary O.S.D., by Rev. H. Collins.
AUGUSTINE MC'NALLY, Tertiary O.S.D., by the Rev. H. Collins.
WILLIE & HIS SISTERS.

☞ Will be followed by others uniform in size and binding.

---

**Father Milleriot, the Ravignan of the Working Men of Paris.** From the French of the Rev. Pere Clair, S.J., with the special permission of the Author, by Mrs. F. Raymond-Barker. Foolscap 8vo, cloth, price 2s.

**Graziella; or the History of a Broken Heart.** An Episode of my Life. By A. De Lamartine. Translated from the French by J. B. S. Foolscap 8vo., cloth elegant, price 2s. 6d.

**Heaven Opened; or, our Home in Heaven,** and the Way Thither. A Manual of Guidance for Devout Souls. By Rev. Father Collins. Post 8vo, handsomely bound, price 5s.

**Legend of the Blessed Virgin Mary,** Mother of Christ our Lord. By Michael Henry Dziewicki. In paper wrapper, price 6d.

# RICHARDSON AND SON'S PUBLICATIONS.
### 23, King Edward Street, City, London; and Derby.

**The Cistercian Fathers,** or Lives and Legends of certain Saints and Blessed of the Order of Citeaux, translated by the Rev. HENRY COLLINS. With a Preface by the Rev. W. R. Brownlow, M.A., one of the Editors of "Roma Sotterranea." First Series, 4s.

**The Cistercian Fathers.** (Second Series.) Translated by Rev. Henry Collins. Price 4s. 6d.

**Visits to the Most Holy Sacrament,** for every Day in the Month; also Preparation for and Thanksgiving after Communion. By S. Alphonsus Liguori. With an Appendix containing Benediction of the Blessed Sacrament. Cloth, price 6d.

**Practice of Christian and Religious Perfection,** by Father Alphonsus Rodriguez, S.J. 3 vols. octavo, cloth, price 12s. the 3 vols.

**BERNADETTE. — Sister Maria-Bernard.** The Sequel to "Our Lady of Lourdes." By HENRI LASSERRE. Translated with the Special Permission of the Author, by MRS. F. RAYMOND-BARKER. Foolscap 8vo, ornamental cloth, price 4s.

**Francis Willington: or, a Life for the Foreign Missions.** By Weston Reay. With a Preface by the Rev. Isaac Moore, S.J. Dedicated by permission to the Bishop of Salford. Crown 8vo, elegantly bound, price 5s.

**Lights and Shadows of Home Affections.** A Moral Tale of the Present Epoch. Humbly Dedicated to her virtuous Queen. By the Authoress of "Footsteps through Life;" "Geraldine," &c. Crown 8vo, elegantly bound, price 7s.

**THE PROBLEM SOLVED. Edited by Lady HERBERT.** Crown 8vo, 450 pp., extra cloth, blocked black, with gold lettering, price 6s.

**MIDDLEFORD HALL.** A Tale for Children. Edited by the Authoress of "ELLERTON PRIORY," "CLAIRE MAITLAND," &c. Handsomely bound in cloth, price 3s.

www.ingramcontent.com/pod-product-compliance
Lightning Source LLC
Chambersburg PA
CBHW022146160426
43197CB00009B/1452